CREATIVE RECIPES FOR

COFFEE

a Salamander book
Published by Salamander Books Limited
LONDON • NEW YORK

Published by Salamander Books Ltd.,
129-137 York Way, London N7 9LG, United Kingdom.

ISBN 0 86101 611 4

Distributed by Hodder and Stoughton Services, PO Box 6, Mill Road, Dunton Green, Sevenoaks, Kent TN13 2XX.

CREDITS

RECIPES BY: *Caroline Cowen, Gordon Grimsdale, Carole Handslip, Lesley Mackley, Janice Murfitt, Lorna Rhodes and Sally Taylor*

PHOTOGRAPHY BY: *Sue Atkinson, Simon Butcher, Per Ericson, David Gill and Paul Grater*

DESIGN BY: *Tim Scott*

TYPESET BY: *Maron Graphics, Wembley*

COLOUR SEPARATION BY: *P & W Graphics, Pte. Ltd.*

PRINTED IN BELGIUM BY: *Proost International Book Production, Turnhout, Belgium*

CONTENTS

ICED MOCHA SOUFFLÉS

4 eggs, separated
125 g (4 oz / ¾ cup) icing sugar, sifted
90 g (3 oz) plain (dark) chocolate, in pieces
1 tablespoon instant coffee powder
315 ml (10 fl oz / 1¼ cups) double (thick) cream
2 tablespoons Kahlua
2 tablespoons grated plain (dark) chocolate

Tie a double band of foil very tightly around 6 ramekin dishes, to stand 2.5 cm (1 in) above rim.

In a bowl, whisk egg yolks and icing sugar together, using an electric whisk until really thick.

Put chocolate, coffee powder and 2 tablespoons water in a small saucepan and heat very gently until melted; cool slightly, then whisk into egg yolk mixture.

In a bowl, whip cream with Kahlua; set aside. In another bowl, whisk egg whites until stiff, then carefully fold into chocolate mixture with three quarters of the cream. Pour into prepared ramekins and freeze overnight. Remove foil carefully and pipe remaining Kahlua cream round the edge of each soufflé. Decorate with grated chocolate and serve immediately. *Serves 6*

COFFEE & CARDAMOM CARAMEL

10 cardamom pods, lightly crushed
625 ml (20 fl oz / 2½ cups) milk
2 eggs
2 egg yolks
45 g (1½ oz / 8 teaspoons) caster sugar
6 teaspoons instant coffee granules
125 g (4 oz / ½ cup) granulated sugar
4 tablespoons water

Preheat the oven to 160C (325F/Gas 3). Place cardamom pods in a saucepan with milk. Heat almost to boiling point, then remove from heat and set aside. Place granulated sugar and water in a heavy-based saucepan. Heat gently until sugar has dissolved, then bring to boil and boil rapidly until golden brown. Pour into six ramekin dishes and set aside. In a large bowl, beat eggs and egg yolks lightly together. Stir in caster sugar. Reheat milk until almost boiling. Add coffee and stir until dissolved. Slowly stir coffee-flavoured milk into egg and sugar mixture. Strain custard into a jug, then carefully pour it into ramekins. Stand ramekins in a roasting pan and pour in enough hot water to come halfway up the side of ramekins. Bake in the oven for about 45 minutes or until set. Remove ramekins from pan and leave to cool. *Serves 6*

COFFEE & RUM SAUCE

125 ml (4 fl oz / ½ cup) hot strong black coffee
2 teaspoons sugar
2 egg yolks
75 ml (2½ fl oz / ⅓ cup) double (thickened) cream
1 teaspoon cornflour
1 tablespoon milk
2 tablespoons dark rum

Place coffee in the top half of a double boiler. Stir in sugar until dissolved, then cool slightly. Add egg yolks, one at a time, combining thoroughly after each addition. Have hot water just below simmering point in the bottom half of the double boiler, and heat coffee mixture. Stir in cream and cook for 1 to 2 minutes.

Mix together cornflour with milk, then add to saucepan and stir constantly until sauce thickens. If serving hot, add rum, stir and serve immediately. If serving cold, allow to cool, stirring occasionally to prevent skin formation. Add rum just before serving. Serve with fresh fruit. *Makes about 250 ml (8 fl oz / 1 cup)*

COFFEE CHIFFON DESSERTS

60 g (2 oz / ¼ cup) butter
9 teaspoons golden syrup
220 g (7 oz / 2 cups) crunchy oat biscuit crumbs
30 g (1 oz / 9 teaspoons) cornflour
60 g (2 oz / ¼ cup) caster sugar
3 teaspoons instant coffee
315 ml (10 fl oz / 1¼ cups) milk
2 eggs, separated
5 teaspoons powdered gelatine
315 ml (10 fl oz / 1¼ cups) whipping cream
155 ml (5 fl oz / ⅔ cup) double (thick) cream, whipped
and liqueur chocolate coffee beans, to decorate

Melt butter and syrup in a saucepan; mix in biscuit crumbs. Divide between 8 moulds, lined with plastic wrap; press over bases and sides. Chill. Blend cornflour with sugar, coffee and milk in a saucepan. Bring to boil, stirring; cook for 2 minutes. Remove from heat; beat in egg yolks. Sprinkle gelatine over 9 teaspoons hot water in a small bowl; leave to soften and dissolve. Stir into coffee mixture; leave until thick. Stiffly whisk egg whites; whip cream until thick. Fold in cream and egg whites. Fill moulds, cover and chill until set. Invert moulds onto plates and serve. Decorate with cream and coffee beans. *Makes 8*

MOCHA TIA MARIA FONDUE

225g (8 oz) plain (dark) chocolate
3 teaspoons instant coffee powder
155 ml (5 fl oz / 2/3 cup) double (thick) cream
3 tablespoons Tia Maria
a selection of fresh fruit, to serve
2 egg whites
125 g (4 oz / 1/2 cup) caster sugar
60 g (2 oz) flaked almonds, lightly toasted

To make meringues, preheat oven to 110C (225F/ Gas 1/4). Line 2 or 3 baking sheets with non-stick paper. Whisk egg whites until stiff, then fold in half the sugar and whisk again until stiff. Lightly fold in remaining sugar. Put teaspoonfuls of mixture onto lined baking sheets to make a total of 30. Insert a few almonds into each one, then bake for 1 1/2-2 hours until dry and crisp. Turn off oven, but leave meringues in oven to cool. Peel meringues off paper once they are cool.

To make mocha fondue, break up chocolate into a fondue pot, add coffee and cream and heat gently until melted, stirring all the time. Stir in Tia Maria and beat until smooth. Leave pot over a burner to keep warm. Serve with nutty meringues and fruit. *Serves 6*

BITTER MOCHA SAUCE

90 g (3 oz) bitter plain (dark) chocolate
1 tablespoon dark, very strong, coarsely ground expresso coffee grounds
315 ml (10 fl oz/1¼ cups) whipping cream
7 g (¼ oz/1½ teaspoons) butter

Break chocolate into small pieces and place in the top of a double boiler or a bowl. Set aside. Put coffee and cream into a saucepan, bring to boil, then remove from heat and leave to infuse for 30 minutes.

Strain creamy coffee through a fine sieve onto the chocolate. Place over a pan of simmering water and stir until chocolate has melted.

Whisk in butter to make sauce glossy and serve at once.
Serves 6-8

Bitter Mocha Sauce can be served with *Coffee Bombe, page 20.*

COFFEE BOMBE

3 eggs, separated
185 g (6 oz / 3/4 cup) caster sugar
75 ml (2½ fl oz / 1/3 cup) cold strong black coffee
500 ml (16 fl oz / 2 cups) double (thick) cream
155 g (5 oz) meringues
whipped cream and chocolate coffee beans, to decorate
hot Bitter Mocha Sauce (see page 18)

In a large bowl, beat egg yolks and sugar together until thick and mousse-like. Gently stir in coffee. In a separate bowl, whip cream lightly. Crush meringues. Fold cream and meringues into coffee mixture. In a large bowl, whisk egg whites until stiff and fold 1 tablespoon into coffee mixture. Tip egg whites onto coffee mixture, then fold together carefully. Pour into a 2 litre (64 fl oz/8 cup) lightly oiled bombe mould and freeze until firm.

One hour before serving, transfer the bombe to the refrigerator to soften slightly. Turn out onto a serving dish and decorate with cream and chocolate coffee beans. Serve with hot Bitter Mocha Sauce handed separately. *Serves 8*

MAPLE PECAN TORTE

125 g (4 oz/¾ cup) light soft brown sugar
4 egg yolks
155 g (5 oz/1⅓ cups) pecan nuts, ground
3 teaspoons dried white breadcrumbs
3 teaspoons strong coffee
3 egg whites, whisked until stiff
315 ml (10 fl oz/1¼ cups) double (thick) cream
3 teaspoons strong black coffee
3-4 tablespoons maple syrup
8 chocolate rose leaves, to decorate

Preheat oven to 180C (350F/Gas 4). Grease and line a 20 cm (8 in) round cake tin. In a bowl, whisk together sugar and egg yolks until thick and light. Fold in ground nuts and breadcrumbs, then stir in coffee. Fold egg whites into mixture. Pour into prepared tin and bake in the oven for 25-30 minutes, until well risen and firm. Cool. For the decoration, brush chocolate over underside of leaves. Place on greaseproof paper and leave until completely set. Peel off. To make filling, in a bowl whip cream and coffee together until thick. Stir in maple syrup. Slice cooled cake horizontally into 2 layers and sandwich together with half the cream. Spread remaining cream over cake and decorate.
Serves 8

RICH MOCHA CAKE

185 g (6 oz) plain (dark) chocolate, in pieces
4 tablespoons cold black coffee
185 g (6 oz) unsalted butter or margarine
185 g (6 oz/1 cup) dark soft brown sugar
4 eggs, separated
125 g (4 oz/1⅓ cups) ground almonds
60 g (2 oz/½ cup) plain flour, sifted
250 g (8 oz/1½ cups) icing sugar, sifted
1 tablespoon coffee essence
8 chocolate-coated nuts, to decorate

Preheat oven to 160C (325F/Gas 3). Grease and line a 20 cm (8 in) round cake tin. Put chocolate and coffee in a small pan and heat gently until chocolate has melted; set aside. In a bowl, beat butter or margarine and brown sugar together until light and fluffy. Beat in egg yolks, one at a time, then beat in chocolate while still warm. Fold in ground almonds and flour. In a bowl, whisk egg whites until fairly stiff. Fold 2 tablespoons into chocolate mixture, then carefully fold in the rest. Turn into tin and bake for 1-1¼ hours. Cool on a wire rack. Place icing sugar in a bowl, add coffee essence and enough water to mix to a thick consistency. Coat the cake. Decorate with chocolate-coated nuts. *Serves 8*

TIRAMI SU

3 eggs
140 g (4½ oz/½ cup + 1 tablespoon) caster sugar
90 g (3 oz/¾ cup) plain flour
3 teaspoons instant coffee powder
375 g (12 oz) mascarpone cheese
4 egg yolks
125 g (4 oz/½ cup) caster sugar
2 tablespoons rum
2 egg whites, whisked until stiff
185 ml (6 fl oz/¾ cup) black coffee
60 g (2 oz) plain (dark) chocolate, grated

To make cake, preheat oven to 180C (350F/Gas 4). Grease and line a 20 cm (8 in) round cake tin. In a bowl, whisk eggs and sugar together until thick and light. Sift flour with coffee powder over mixture, then fold in. Bake mixture in the oven for 30 minutes, until golden. Cool. In a bowl beat mascarpone until soft. In another bowl, whisk egg yolks and sugar until thick and light. Stir in mascarpone and rum. Fold in egg whites. Cut cake into 3 layers. Put one layer on a plate. Sprinkle with one third of the coffee. Cover with one third of the filling. Repeat, finishing with a topping of cheese mixture. Chill overnight. Sprinkle with grated chocolate to serve. *Serves 8*

NEGRESSE EN CHEMISE

185 g (6 oz) plain (dark) chocolate
5 tablespoons strong black coffee
185 g (6 oz / ¾ cup) unsalted butter
185 g (6 oz / ¾ cup) caster sugar
5 large eggs, beaten
375 ml (12 fl oz / 1½ cups) whipping cream

Preheat oven to 180C (350F/Gas 4). Line a 1 litre (32 fl oz/4 cup) pudding bowl or soufflé dish with double thickness of foil.

Melt chocolate with coffee in top of a double boiler or a bowl set over a saucepan of simmering water. Gradually beat in butter and sugar and heat until mixture is hot. Remove from heat and gradually whisk in eggs. Strain mixture into prepared dish, cover with foil and place in a roasting tin. Add boiling water to tin to come halfway up dish, then bake in the oven for 65 minutes, until top has a thick crust. Cool, then refrigerate.

When ready to serve, unmould pudding onto a serving dish and peel away foil carefully. In a bowl, whip cream stiffly, then cover the cake with two-thirds of it. Use remainder to pipe cream rosettes round top edge and base of cake. *Serves 6-8*

PECAN PIE

185 g (6 oz / 1½ cups) plain flour
100 g (3½ oz) unsalted butter
3 teaspoons caster sugar
1 egg yolk, beaten with 3 teaspoons water
155 ml (5 fl oz / ⅔ cup) maple syrup
125 g (4 oz / ½ cup) demerara sugar
3 eggs
2 tablespoons instant coffee granules, dissolved in 1 tablespoon hot milk
185 g (6 oz / 1½ cups) pecan nuts

To make pastry, sift flour into a bowl, rub in butter until mixture resembles breadcrumbs, then stir in caster sugar. Stir in beaten egg yolk. Knead lightly to form a firm dough. Cover and chill for 30 minutes.

Preheat oven to 190C (375F/Gas 5). On a lightly floured surface, roll out pastry and use to line a 20 cm (8 in) flat tin.

To make filling, in a saucepan, heat together maple syrup and demerara sugar until sugar has dissolved; leave to cool slightly. In a bowl, beat together eggs and coffee-flavoured milk; stir in maple syrup mixture and nuts. Pour into prepared flan case and bake in the oven for 30-40 minutes, until filling has set. Serve warm or cold, with cream or vanilla ice cream. *Serves 6-8*

COFFEE ALMOND SHORTCAKE

250 g (8 oz/2 cups) plain flour
185 g (6 oz) unsalted butter
125 g (4 oz/½ cup) caster sugar
185 g (6 oz/⅔ cup) ground almonds
90 g (3 oz/⅓ cup) caster sugar
90 g (3 oz/½ cup) icing sugar
1 egg yolk
2 teaspoons coffee essence
30 g (1 oz/2 tablespoons) blanched almonds, to decorate

Preheat oven to 160C (325F/Gas 3). Butter a 23 cm (9 in) loose-based flan tin. To make shortbread, sift flour into a bowl, rub in butter, then stir in caster sugar. Knead until firm. To make marzipan, in a bowl, mix together ground almonds, caster sugar and icing sugar. Stir in egg yolk and coffee essence. On a lightly floured surface, roll out marzipan to form a circle slightly smaller than the diameter of the tin. Divide shortbread into 2, one piece slightly larger than the other. Roll out the larger piece and press over base and side of tin. Lay marzipan on top. Roll out second piece of dough to fit tin and place on top of marzipan; seal edges firmly. Press almonds on top of shortcake. Bake for 45-50 minutes until golden. Cool in tin. Remove and serve in wedges. *Serves 6-8*

COFFEE & CARAWAY ROLLS

375 g (12 oz/3 cups) strong white bread flour
1 teaspoon salt
2 teaspoons 'easy blend' dried yeast
2 teaspoons caraway seeds
60 g (2 oz) butter
185 ml (6 fl oz/¾ cup) milk
6 teaspoons instant coffee granules
1 teaspoon caster sugar
1 egg, beaten and
1 teaspoon caraway seeds, to glaze

Grease a baking sheet. Sift flour and salt into a bowl. Stir in yeast and caraway seeds. In a small saucepan, gently heat butter, milk and coffee until combined and lukewarm. Add sugar and stir until dissolved. Make a well in centre of flour, pour in liquid ingredients and mix together thoroughly. Knead dough. Put in a large bowl, cover loosely with plastic wrap and leave to rise in a warm place for about 2 hours. Knead again for 2-3 minutes. Divide dough into 8, roll each one into a thin 'sausage' and knot in the centre. Place on prepared baking sheet, cover and leave to rise for 45 minutes. Preheat oven to 200C (400F/Gas 6). Brush rolls with beaten egg and sprinkle with caraway seeds. Bake in the oven for 15-20 minutes. *Makes 8*

PALMIERS

250 g (8 oz) puff pastry, thawed if frozen
caster sugar for dredging
60 g (2 oz / ¼ cup) caster sugar
3 teaspoons instant coffee powder

Preheat oven to 190C (375F/Gas 5). Roll out pastry to a 30.5 × 20 cm (12 × 8 in) rectangle on a surface dredged with caster sugar.

In a bowl, mix together sugar and coffee powder. Sprinkle half of this mixture over pastry. Fold long edges of pastry into middle, then fold long sides together.

On sugared surface, roll pastry out again to same size. Sprinkle with remaining sugar and coffee mixture. Fold long edges into middle, fold into middle again, then press together with a rolling pin. Cut dough into 1 cm (½ in) pieces. Put on baking sheets, allowing room for spreading, and flatten slightly. Bake in the oven for 15-20 minutes, turning over halfway through cooking time. until crisp and golden. Remove from baking sheets immediately and cool on wire racks. *Makes 30*

COFFEE CREAMS

500 g (1 lb/2 cups) granulated sugar
pinch of cream of tartar
9 teaspoons single (light) cream
½ teaspoon coffee essence
90 g (3 oz) plain (dark) chocolate, to finish

Put sugar in a heavy-based pan, add 155 ml (5 fl oz/⅔ cup) water and heat gently until sugar has dissolved. Bring to the boil. Add cream of tartar. Boil until syrup registers 116C (240F) on a sugar thermometer or until a few drops of syrup form a soft ball when dropped into a cup of cold water. Stir in cream.

Sprinkle a little water on a work surface or marble board. Pour syrup onto surface or board and leave for a few minutes to cool. When a skin forms around the edges, collect syrup together with a spatula. Turn mixture, working it backwards and forwards in a figure of 8 movement, until it becomes opaque and grainy, then knead in coffee essence. Roll small pieces of fondant into a ball, then press to flatten slightly. Leave overnight to dry.

To finish, melt chocolate in a bowl placed over a pan of hot water. Dip one end of each coffee cream into chocolate to half-coat. Leave on non-stick paper to dry. *Makes 20*

BRANDY COFFEE CUPS

155 g (5 oz) plain (dark) chocolate, in pieces
1 teaspoon sunflower oil
155 ml (5 fl oz / ⅔ cup) double (thick) cream
3 teaspoons instant coffee powder
185 g (6 oz) white chocolate, in small pieces
2 teaspoons brandy

To make chocolate cases, put chocolate and oil in a bowl placed over a pan of hot water. Leave until melted, then stir until smooth. Spread melted chocolate evenly over inside of 20 double thickness petit four cases. Chill until set. Re-melt chocolate, if necessary. Spread a second layer of chocolate in cases. Chill until completely set. Carefully remove paper cases.

To make filling, in a saucepan heat cream and coffee powder to boiling point, stirring until coffee has dissolved; remove from heat. Add white chocolate and stir until smooth. Return to low heat and stir until mixture begins to bubble. Gradually stir in brandy. Set aside to cool.

Beat chocolate cream until thick. Spoon into a piping bag fitted with a large star nozzle and pipe into the chocolate cases. Store in the refrigerator. Use within 2-3 days. *Makes 20*

COFFEE COCKTAILS

CAFÉ ALEXANDER

crushed ice
6 teaspoons strong black coffee, chilled and sweetened to taste
6 teaspoons crème de cacao
8 teaspoons brandy
6 teaspoons double (thick) cream, chilled
chocolate curls

Put crushed ice into a cocktail shaker. Add coffee, crème de cacao, brandy and cream. Shake well; strain into a glass. Top with chocolate curls to serve. *Serves 1*

GAELIC COFFEE

1 teaspoon demerara sugar
6 teaspoons Irish whiskey
125 ml (4 fl oz / ½ cup) hot freshly made coffee
6 teaspoons double (thick) cream

Put sugar in a heatproof glass; add whiskey. Pour in coffee. Dip a teaspoon into the coffee to warm it, then carefully pour cream over back of spoon to float on the coffee. For *Jamaican Coffee,* substitute dark rum for whiskey and sprinkle grated nutmeg over cream. *Serves 1*

COFFEE COCKTAILS

CAFÉ BRULÔT

4 cloves
strip of lemon and orange rind
½ cinnamon stick
3 teaspoons demerara sugar
60 ml (2 fl oz / ¼ cup) brandy
500 ml (16 fl oz / 2 cups) hot freshly made coffee

In a bowl, put cloves, lemon and orange peel, cinnamon and sugar. In a ladle, warm brandy; ignite and pour into bowl. Stir until sugar has dissolved. Slowly pour in hot coffee, stirring. Ladle into warmed cups. For *Café de Olla*, replace citrus peel and brandy with 5 cm (2 in) stick cinnamon. *Serves 4*

ALMOND COFFEE

1 teaspoon demerara sugar
6 teaspoons Amaretto
125 ml (4 fl oz / ½ cup) hot freshly made coffee
whipped cream and 1 teaspoon slivered almonds, to serve

Put sugar and Amaretto in a heatproof glass. Pour in coffee. Top with cream and sprinkle with almonds. *Serves 1*